BLUEFISHING

Acknowledgment and Dedication

Tommy Shute, a South Jersey commercial fisherman, used to take me along with him when I was young and eager to learn everything about fish. The late Franklin Watkins, a Philadelphia portrait painter, taught me a lot about surf-fishing for blues. Hal Lyman, the publisher of *Salt Water Sportsman,* has given me tips and his magazine and books are full of useful information. And then there were the anglers who were eager to share their knowledge — most of them were polite; the others at least let me watch.

This book is for everyone interested in bluefish, and that's a long, long list.

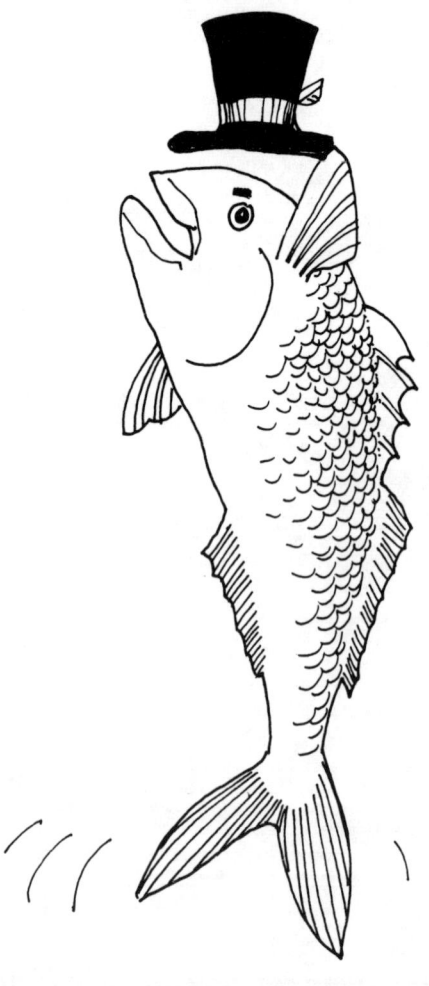

Secrets Of Bluefishing

by D.W. Bennett

ISBN 0-88839-086-6

Copyright © 1982 D.W. Bennett

Cataloging in Publication Data.

Bennett, D.W.
  Secrets of bluefishing
  (North East fishing series)

  1. Bluefish. 2. Bluefishing. I. Title.
  II. Series.
  SH691.B55B45   799.1'758   C81-091018-7

All rights reserved. No part of this publication may be reproduced, stored in a retrieval system or transmitted, in any form or by any means, electronic, mechanical, photocopying, recording or otherwise, without the prior written permission of Hancock House Publishers.

Editor Margaret Campbell
Typeset by Anne Whatcott in Garamond type on an AM Varityper Comp/Edit
Layout Linda Rourke
Production & Cover Design Peter Burakoff
Artwork by Barb Wood
Printed by Friesen Printers, Altona, Manitoba, Canada

Front Cover Photo: Al Ristori
Back Cover Photos (Top): Al Ristori
              (Bottom) Dery W. Bennett

Hancock House Publishers
256 Route 81, Killingworth, CT, U.S.A. 06417
Hancock House Publishers Ltd.
19313 Zero Avenue, Surrey, B.C., Canada V3S 5J9

Secrets Of Bluefishing

Table of Contents

   Secrets of Bluefishing 4
1. Bluefishing from Boats 14
2. Bait for Bluefish 33
3. Surf-fishing for Bluefish 36
4. Snappers 47
5. Keeping and Cleaning Your Catch 51
6. Cooking Bluefish 60
   In Conclusion 71

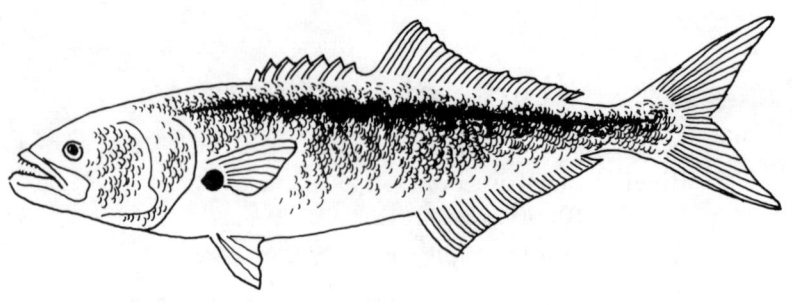

Secrets of Bluefishing

About Bluefish

Bluefish *(Pomatomus saltatrix)* are robust, predatory saltwater fish. They live in the temperate and warm-temperate waters over the Atlantic continental shelf. Their range is extensive: from Canada south to Florida, along the Gulf coast, and along the coast of South America to Uruguay. On the eastern side of the Atlantic, they range from Portugal south along the African coast to Senegal. They are found in the Mediterranean and Black Seas, and are even found "down under," where bluefish are common along nearly the entire coasts of Australia and New Zealand.

In short, bluefish are widely known everywhere except in the Pacific Ocean, and they are rarely found far from the land's edge.

Bluefish found along the east coast of the United States are born in the waters off New Jersey, Maryland, Virginia, the Carolinas, and possibly as far south as Florida. Spawning occurs in the spring and early summer (May through July).

Small bluefish, about an inch long, arrive on the coast within weeks after spawning and enter inlets all along the shore, where they feed voraciously on small fish and shrimp. The young bluefish can grow as much as one inch every week.

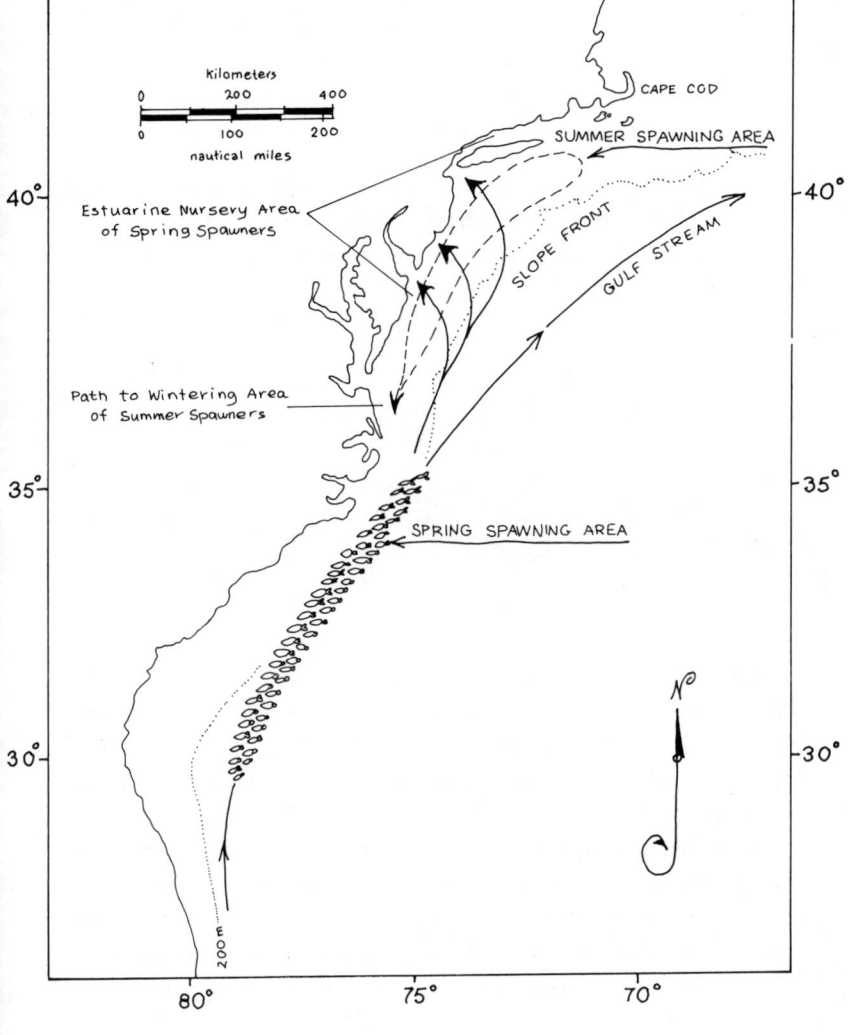

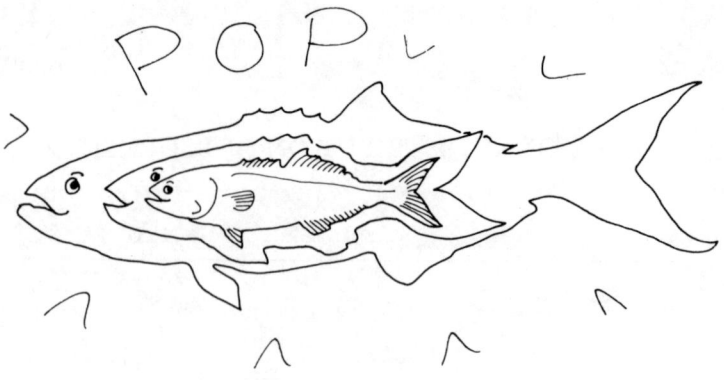

Larger fish may also enter estuaries in the summer, stop and feed, and then move on. I have tangled with bluefish as large as ten pounds, way up rivers in the dead of summer. They were feeding on four-inch bluefish.

In the fall, when water temperatures drop, the bluefish leave the estuaries and move south and offshore for the winter. Most bluefish have moved south of New England and the mid-Atlantic area by the middle of October, although there always seems to be a late fall catch reported offshore in November.

As you would expect from the name, bluefish are blue, or at least partly so. The top of the fish tends to be light blue-gray, but sometimes looks green. The body is a lighter silvery color toward the sides and belly. Bluefish have large mouths, sharp teeth, and large eyes — they feed mostly by sight. There is usually a dark spot near the base of the pectoral fin (the fin right behind the gills on each side of the fish). Bluefish look somewhat like pompano, but they are longer, thinner, and their scales are bigger.

The bluefish born in the summer is about five to eight inches long by the fall and weighs about a third of a pound. By age two, a bluefish is about fourteen inches long and weighs a pound and a half. (See following chart.)

AGE	WEIGHT (POUNDS)	LENGTH (INCHES)
three	three	eighteen
five	seven	twenty-five
seven	eleven	twenty-nine

After age seven, growth slows considerably.

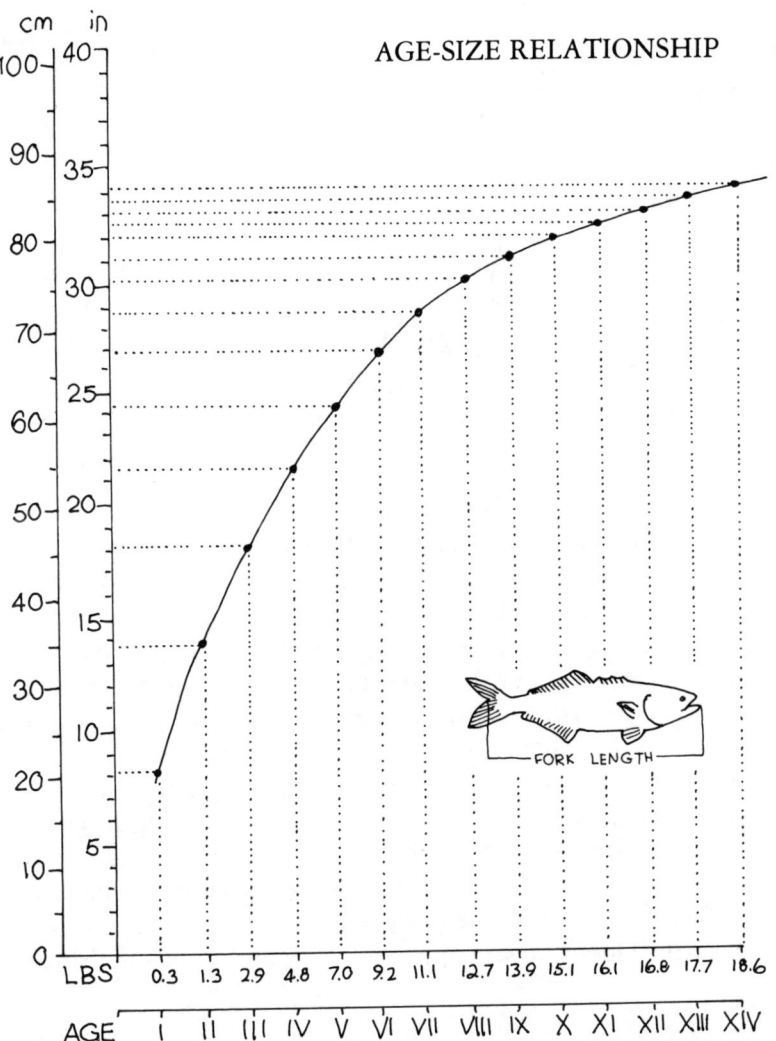

The world's record bluefish was caught in North Carolina on January 30, 1972. It weighed thirty-one and three-quarter pounds and broke the previous record by a hefty five pounds.

Most bluefish caught in rivers and bays during the summer are around six inches long. Surf-caught bluefish weigh from one to four pounds. Larger fish are most often caught farther offshore.

Like many fish, bluefish are subject to extreme variations in population. Back in the 1930s, any bluefish caught in the northeast was a rarity. In 1945, small bluefish began appearing in greater numbers, and one-pound blues were being caught in 1946 through 1948. Since then, bluefish have been common along the Atlantic coast, and an increase in the size of bluefish has been noted. While it was unusual twenty-five years ago to see many bluefish over ten pounds, now twenty-pound fish are common.

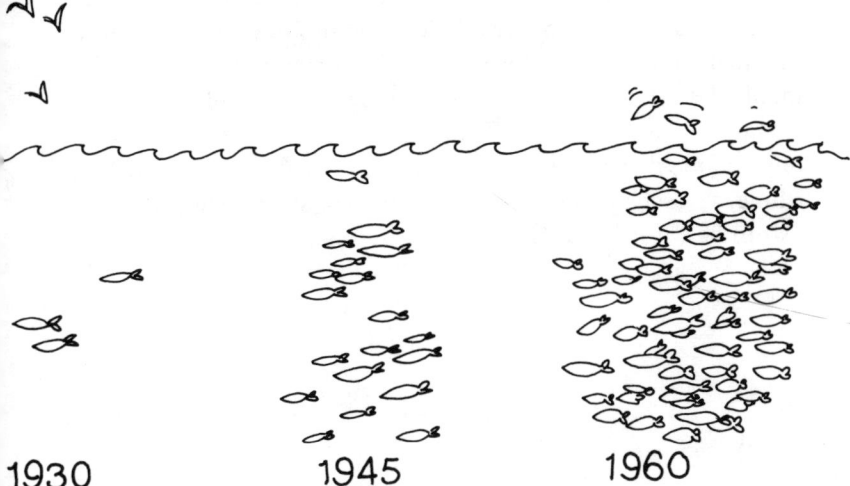

Bluefish have many different names, depending on the locality. Small bluefish (one pound and under) are called snapper blues or snappers. Fish weighing one or two pounds that are caught in bays are sometimes called harbor blues or tailors. And bluefish of all sizes can be called blues, fatbacks, snap mackerel, choppers, horse mackerel, or skip mackerel. Big bluefish caught in the Carolinas in late fall are sometimes called Hatteras blues, but the most common name for all varieties is bluefish or blue.

Bluefish are predators. They are known to move and feed in large schools driving baitfish before them, sometimes right into the surf and onto the beach. Their favorite food is fish — menhaden (bunkers), mullet, minnows, mackerel, sand eels, anchovies, juvenile fish of any kind, and even large fish. A ten-pound bluefish has no trouble eating a one-pound fish whole, and such blues have been known to simply chop a bigger fish in half if it is too large to take in one gulp.

Sometimes a school of feeding bluefish can be seen from a distance, churning and splashing the water, while the baitfish leap out of the water to avoid the bluefish's teeth. The bluefish themselves may jump clear of the water in search of a meal. When this happens, gulls and terns will often accompany the school, diving into it from the air. The unfortunate baitfish are caught in the middle.

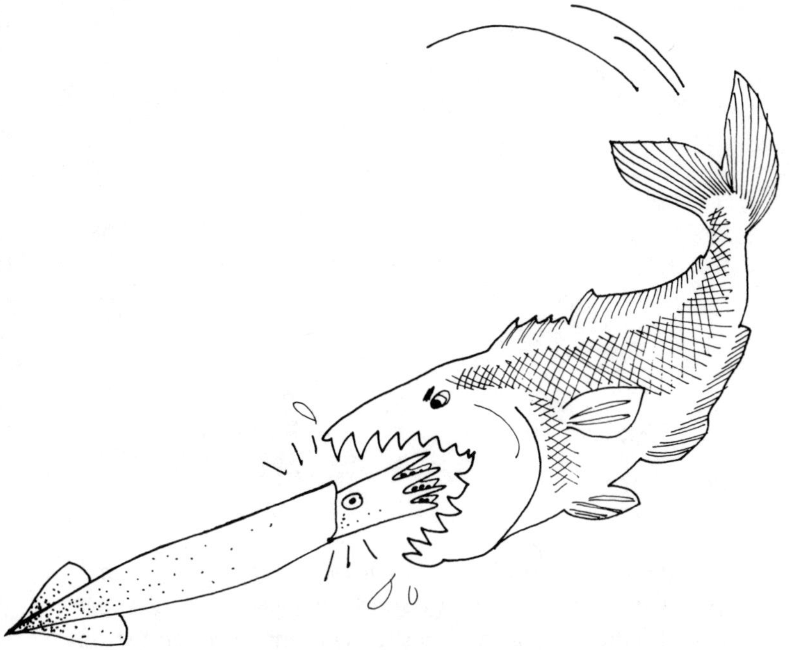

Bluefish will feed on the bottom, too, chasing squid and fish or snapping up worms. Evidence that bluefish feed on more than 100 different kinds of food have been found.

As mentioned before, bluefish have very sharp teeth and strong jaws, so remember: treat all bluefish with caution when unhooking them. Even a snapper can draw blood with ease, and a larger fish can cause real damage. A bluefish lying in the bottom of a boat or on the sand will slash out at passing fingers and toes! **Handle bluefish with care.**

Like many sport fish of the northeast, bluefish are summer fish, spending their winters in southern waters or offshore. Commercial fishermen sometimes trawl them from the bottom off the Virginia Capes, but the first real sign of feeding fish is usually in May when big fish show up inshore, chunky and hungry. There is often a week or so of furious fishing and then a sudden drop in the action. The theory is that the fish feed actively after wintering but move offshore again to spawn in late May through mid-June. Then lean, famished bluefish begin to populate the waters from Chesapeake Bay north to Cape Cod, and in some summers, up as far as Maine where a run of big bluefish surprises natives, some of whom have never seen bluefish until that first invasion.

Boats can get bluefish consistently through the summer; the concentration of fishermen and fish is heaviest off New Jersey, Long Island, Rhode Island, and the lower Cape. The Chesapeake fills up with bluefish. These big fish, over five pounds, come into the surf sporadically through the summer, a one-day blitz here, then gone for a week or more. At the same time, smaller fish, one-pounders, begin to show up more regularly beginning in late August, and they are common along the beaches through October. This is also the time when the big fish will get into the surf for more extended periods. And by then snappers are in the surf too, having spent their summers in the estuaries feeding on small stuff.

While it is possible to catch bluefish of varying sizes on one trip, it is more usual to catch fish that are all about the same size. This is not hard to understand, for a six-inch snapper is just a snack for a five-pound blue. Like many fish, bluefish tend to school by size.

There are beaches and offshore spots that will produce consistent bluefishing in the fall months even when no fish show themselves by feeding near the surface. Best bet is to learn those spots by finding them yourself or asking around. I have one surf spot that I have tried to fish each fall, usually in mid-October, and usually with cut mullet. In more than a dozen years, I have caught fish on every occasion but a few, all fish caught within 100 yards of each other, all caught on the same rod, reel, and line, with the same bait, and all fish about the same size.

It is this sort of "routine" that you should try to establish. Try to figure the fish and where they will be. The longer you stick to it, the better your chances of success will be.

Bluefish can be caught with just about anything, just about anywhere. They can be caught in New York Harbor with tugboats all around, or on a deserted Cape Cod beach. They can be caught at the eastern end of Long Island Sound in a current of five knots, or in the still water of a coastal bay. You can catch them in the middle of the day by fishing from a bridge in downtown Jupiter, Florida, or in the middle of the night eight miles off the coast of Maryland. They can be caught on hot summer days or during October nor'easters.

But let's start with the safest way to assure a catch — going out on a boat that specializes in bluefish.

1. BLUEFISHING FROM BOATS

Bluefishing on Party Boats

Most seashore communities have harbors or docks for party boats, or "head" boats as they are sometimes called. These are large boats that take people out for a day or a half-day of fishing for a fee. Trips usually last eight hours (or four for a half-day boat), cost from $10-$25 per person (per "head"), and carry from twenty to one hundred people. If you are really new at the game, just show up at the dock and look for a boat with a sign that reads "Blues," "Bluefish," or "Chumming Blues," and climb aboard. The boat boats provide bait (part of the price), tackle (usually extra), and instruction. You can find boat names, locations, and schedules in the sport section of local papers, in weekly fishing magazines and newspapers, or by simply checking at the dock the day before you want to go out. In fact, it is great fun to show up at a fishing dock around 4:00 p.m. to watch the boats unload fish and fishermen.

Remember, catching fish is *not* a sure thing, but captains make money by finding fish for their customers. They are usually good at it or they would go out of business.

Party boats have mates, often youngsters working for the summer. They will outfit you with a rod, reel, and tackle, and will help bait hooks and land fish. A good mate deserves a tip at the end of the day.

Many party boats chum; that is, toss chopped fish over-board to attract blues. Then, you will bait with a larger piece of fish and let it drift back into the "chum slick." Sometimes bluefish will stay down deep below the chum. If this happens, weights can be added to the line.

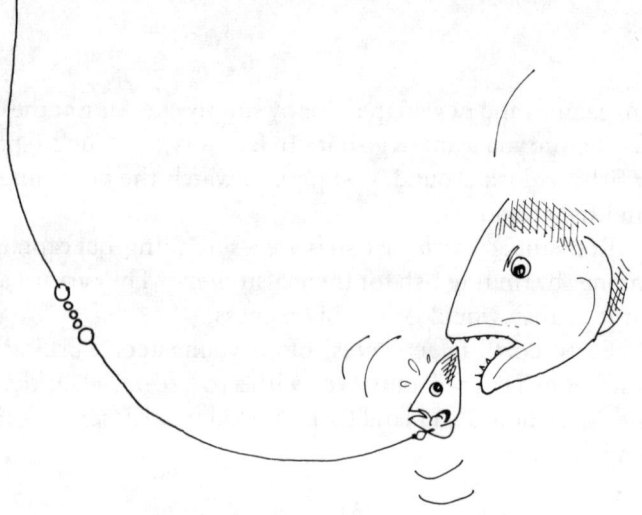

Some fishermen will switch to artificial lures and either cast them out from the boat and reel them back fast, or drop the lure down near the bottom and jig it up and down a foot or so. In both cases, the fisherman is imitating a bait fish by moving the lure.

If you decide to bring along your own fishing equipment, I suggest the following for party boat fishing:
-- a fairly heavy, six- to seven-foot rod
-- a conventional reel (not a spinning reel), equipped with thirty- to forty-pound test line
-- one dozen hooks: sizes 4/0 through 6/0

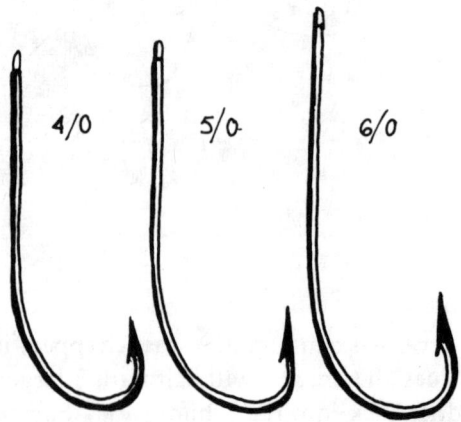

Actual size

-- an assortment of wire and monofilament leaders (sometimes bluefish will shy away from heavy, visible leaders)
-- an assortment of weights: two, three, and four ounce
-- an assortment of lures: three- to six-ounce diamond jigs, some heavy bucktails, and some tube-type, "banana" lures (try for a mixture of colors).

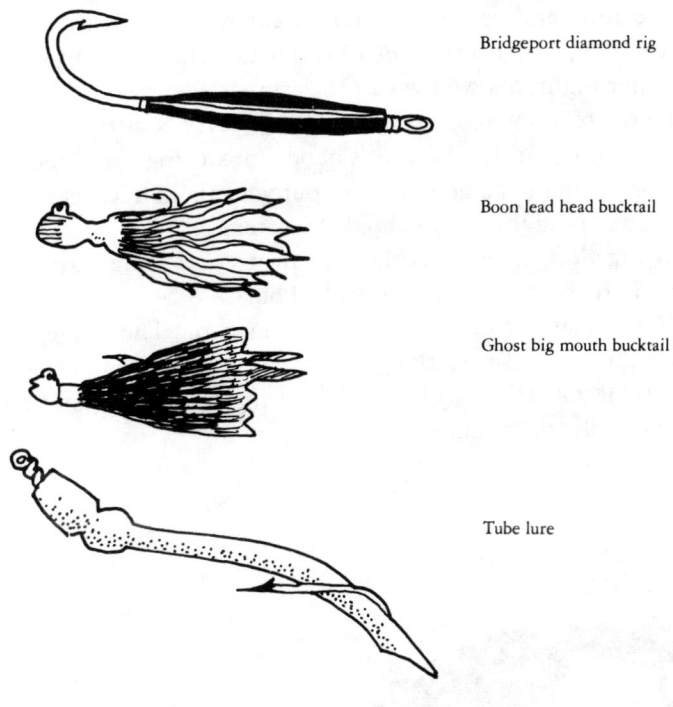

Bridgeport diamond rig

Boon lead head bucktail

Ghost big mouth bucktail

Tube lure

With the heavy rod and line, you can "horse in" big bluefish without tangling up other fishermen's lines. This is important on a crowded party boat. Many of the large party boats sell tackle on board.

A useful trick with any kind of fishing is to watch what the successful fishermen are doing and follow their leads. Sometimes it is only a matter of fishing a lure or bait at a different depth. Other times you will need to change lures or leaders, or the way you are moving your lure or bait. Don't be shy about copying successful techniques.

Here's another tip: if no one is catching anything — and that does happen — then you should try something different. Drop your line near the bottom, or jig faster or slower. At any rate, change your tactics; often it pays off in fish.

Some party boats go after bluefish at night, leaving the dock at suppertime and returning after midnight. It is an interesting way to fish, and if you haven't been out on the ocean on a warm summer night, it's well worth the trip.

Here are a few more suggestions for party boat fishing:

-- Take along an ice chest. It's handy for storing your lunch and drinks, and it's a good idea to put your fish on ice as soon as they are caught (more about this later).

-- Bring along a hat and other sun protection. The glare of the sun off the water can cause a bad burn.

-- Party boats often operate a betting pool. The biggest fish caught wins. Bring along a few extra dollars and join in the fun. If you are lucky, you might bring home a mess of blues and a mess of money!

Bluefishing on Charter Boats

The major difference between a party boat and a charter boat is that you simply show up on the dock for a party boat, pay the fare, and go fishing. On a charter boat, you rent the whole boat. Charter boats are usually smaller; they have a captain, usually a mate, and take up to eight fishermen. Often charter boats chum for bluefish, but usually they troll (trolling is covered later).

Charter boats cost up to $500 a day, but you get much more attention from the captain and crew, and have more say about your schedule. Charter boats almost always provide all fishing tackle, usually in great variety. They are often booked months in advance, especially in summertime, so make your reservations early.

Because there are fewer people fishing on a charter boat than on a party boat, you can use light tackle. There are not as many lines in the water on a charter boat, so you can play your fish without worrying so much about tangling lines. There is no need to "horse in" your blues. It's halfway between party boat fishing and fishing on your own.

Bluefishing on Your Own Boat

Of course, you can buy or rent your own boat and go out after bluefish. Now you are the captain, the mate, and the chief fishing expert. Here are a few tips:

-- Check with local fishermen. Find out where the bluefish were yesterday so you can at least start near where they might be today. Or, once offshore, look for other boats.

-- If you are fishing around other boats, especially party boats that are chumming, be sure to give them plenty of room. Nothing makes a party boat captain angrier than other boats horning in on a chum slick he has made for his customers. Boats already fishing should not be disturbed.

-- Don't cut through a chum slick, and don't cut through a school of feeding fish; the school will scatter or go deep, and no one will catch fish.

-- When trolling (see below), remember that other trollers may have long lines out; again, give other boats plenty of room.

--Even if you are not out specifically to catch fish (perhaps you are just running up the coast for a visit or across the bay for a swim) take some fishing equipment in the boat in case you run across a school of feeding blues. I know some sailors, the real kind with sails on their boats, who even have a handline and some spoons on board when they are racing. If they spot fish close to their racing course, they will take a little extra jog to try a spoon out on the school. They might lose first prize, but they figure second prize and dinner is even better.

--There will be days when you have set out to catch blues and no one else is out fishing, or they are but no fish are coming over the side. It has all the makings of a bad day. Treat this as a challenge. Look for blues. There are a number of approaches.

First, scan the horizon; look for feeding birds. Any sign of bird activity is worth a check. A flock of birds wheeling and diving is the best sign of fish. If you see them, head over there, but be sure to slow down and move with care once you get near the action.

Also, check any flock of gulls sitting on the water. They may have been feeding on a school that has dropped into deeper water or moved off. Wait for the flock to rise and find the school of blues again. Or try casting or jigging under the birds, letting the lure sink halfway or all the way to the bottom. The blues might be down there skulking.

A school of feeding bluefish offshore can move very fast, surging to the surface to feed as a group for a few minutes, then scattering or sounding, and regrouping on the surface again minutes or tens of minutes later in the same place or a mile away. When the school stops feeding, but keeps moving, the birds will often stop diving but will move with the school. Treat gulls like bloodhounds on the track of prey. They will seldom steer you wrong.

What if there are no birds? Look for any disturbance on the water's surface. This can be a sign of feeding fish or the sign of a pair of currents coming together, creating a rough patch of water. Fish any "unnatural" looking piece of water.

If you are inshore and nothing is happening, head offshore. If you're out six miles without a hit, come back in toward the beach. In other words, change location.

Check your charts and head for an uneven bottom or a place where the water shoals up. A flat, even bottom forty feet down is less likely to produce fish than a rolling bottom, or the edge of a channel, a reef, or what is sometimes called a "lump," a hill on the ocean floor.

Fishing right in on the beach is often productive. Many beaches have a sandbar anywhere from 25 to 100 yards from the surf line. Bluefish will often hang on this bar or just off the seaweed edge. Of course, they will also go in across the bar and feed almost into the waves' wash.

You can follow them as long as you are confident enough to handle your boat in tricky water, but take care. There is nothing so frightening as getting caught by an extra big wave close to shore. Each summer the beaches of the northeast provide the final resting place for a number of boats whose captains have tried to get "just a little closer in."

--When you are moving from one place to another, try trolling between spots. Often when fish are showing nowhere, a slowly trolled lure will dig up a blue for you.

--If you have a depth recorder, sometimes called a fish-finder or a fish machine or simply a sounder, get to know its signals and use it to find fish. There are two basic kinds, those that send an impulse down to the bottom and record the answering echo with a flashing light, and those that actually record the profile of the bottom on the paper.

The flasher systems are cheaper than the others, but they have two disadvantages. First, they don't record. That is they don't give you a printed record of what the bottom is like. And second, you need to watch them to see not only the mark of the bottom, but the marks between the boat and the bottom, marks that might mean fish. Here is how a flasher and a recorder show fish and bottom.

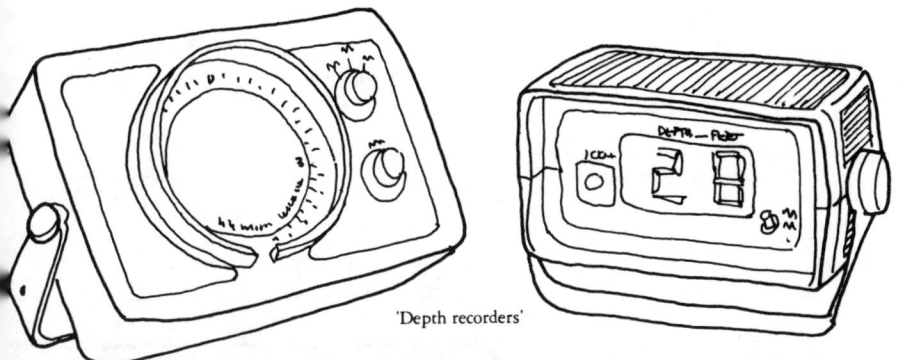

'Depth recorders'

Flasher Readings

A hard bottom shows as a bright, narrow band. On a soft bottom, the mud absorbs some of the signal and the display flash is weaker.

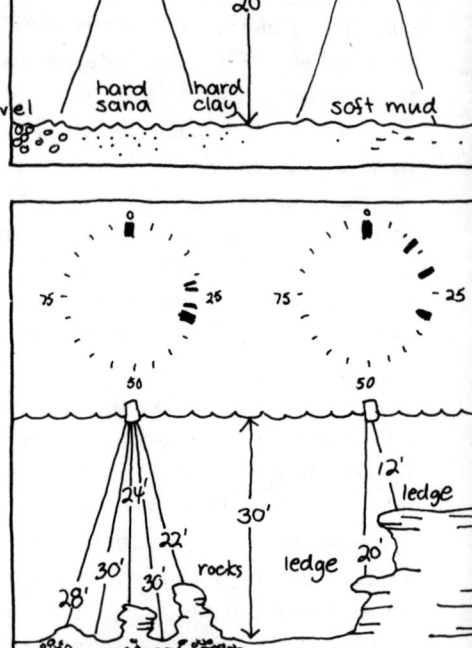

The lowest flash is hard bottom. Momentary flashes indicate tops of rocks. Rock projections register as bright bands.

Flashes from fish are usually not as strong as those from rocks and appear as fine lines or a red smear.

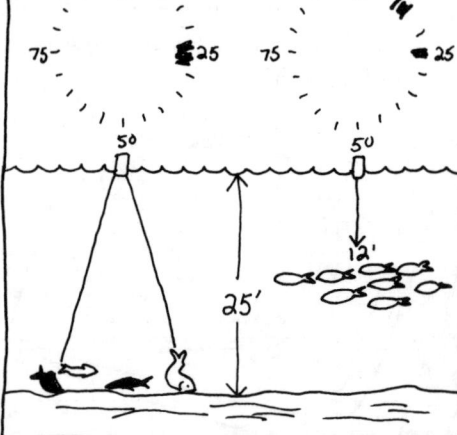

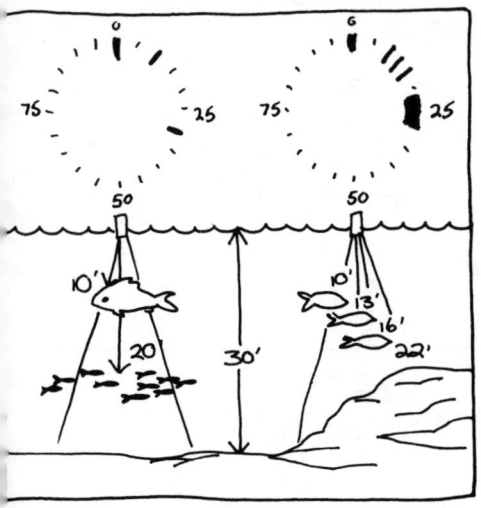

You can often tell the size of fish by the flashes they make.

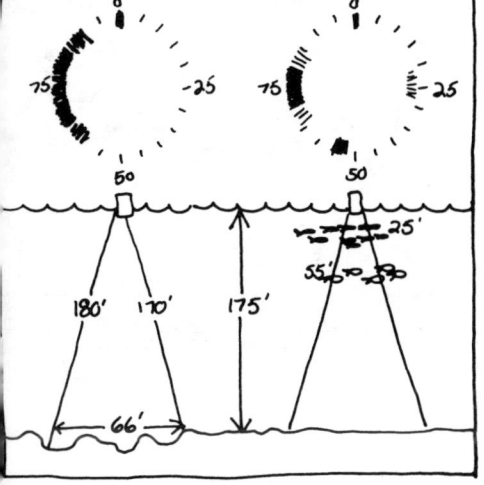

Great depth causes the bottom flash to spread.

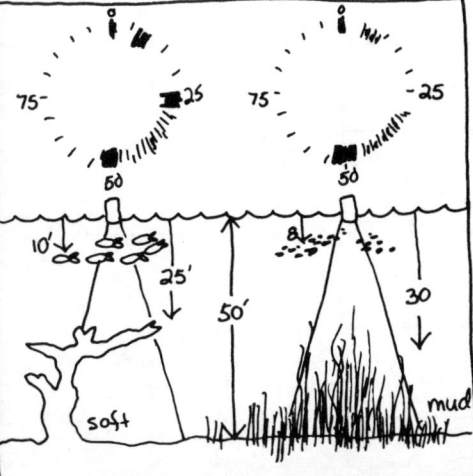

The wide band shows soft bottom. The submerged tree at 25 feet is distinct. The shading over the bottom is submerged tall grass. Large fish in the bottom grass would show as momentary bright flashes of red.

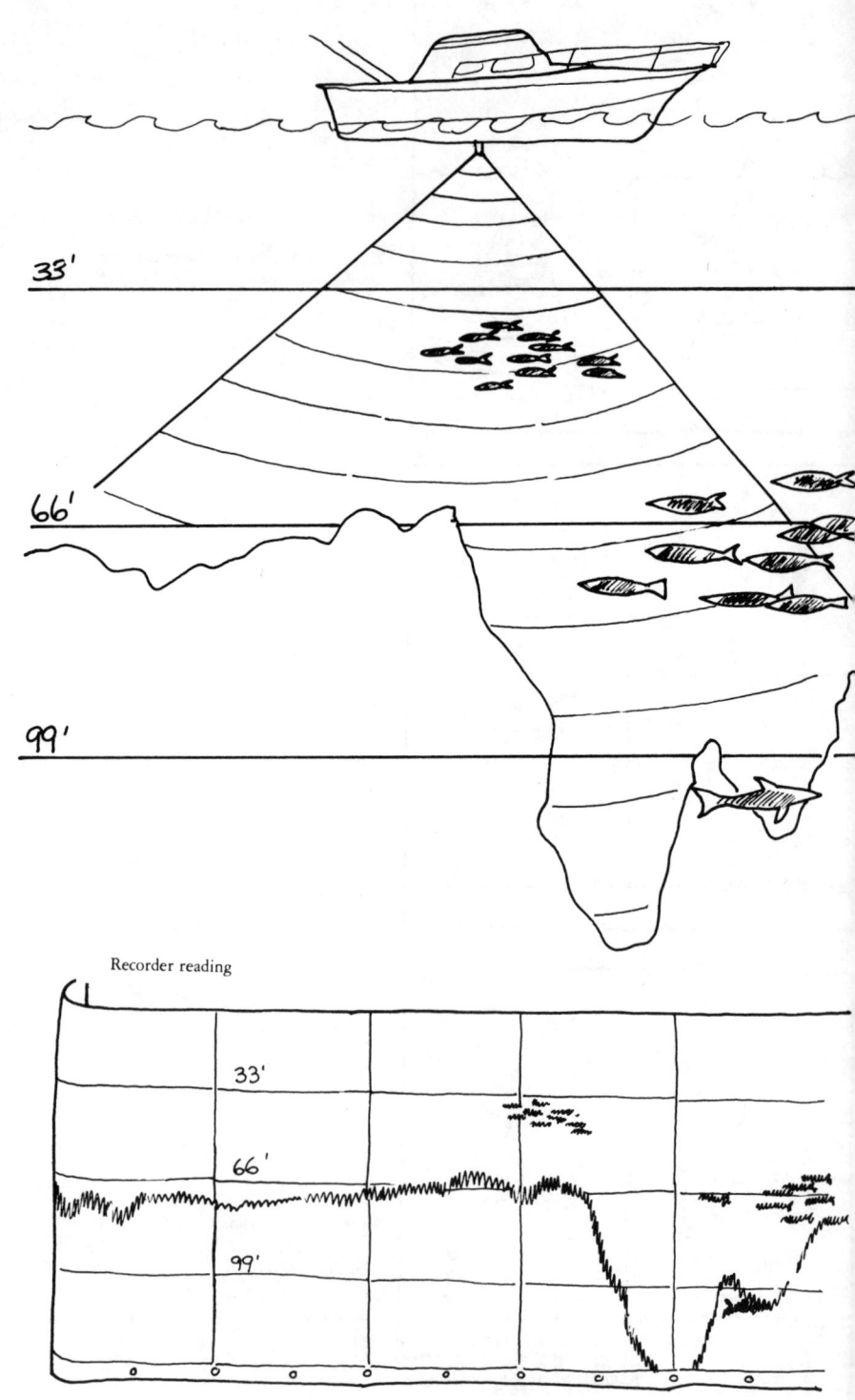

As you gain experience with your recorders you will be able to distinguish bait (faint, cloudy gray marks) from bluefish (dark more distinct marks). Try keeping a written log of readings, or scribble notes right on the recording paper. Note what the mark looked like when you caught the blues, note the depth, and note the look of the bottom and of the fish.

Trolling for Bluefish

Trolling is just like casting except you let the boat do the work. You put out your lines with lures, then drag or troll the lures through the water.

Some trolling weights:

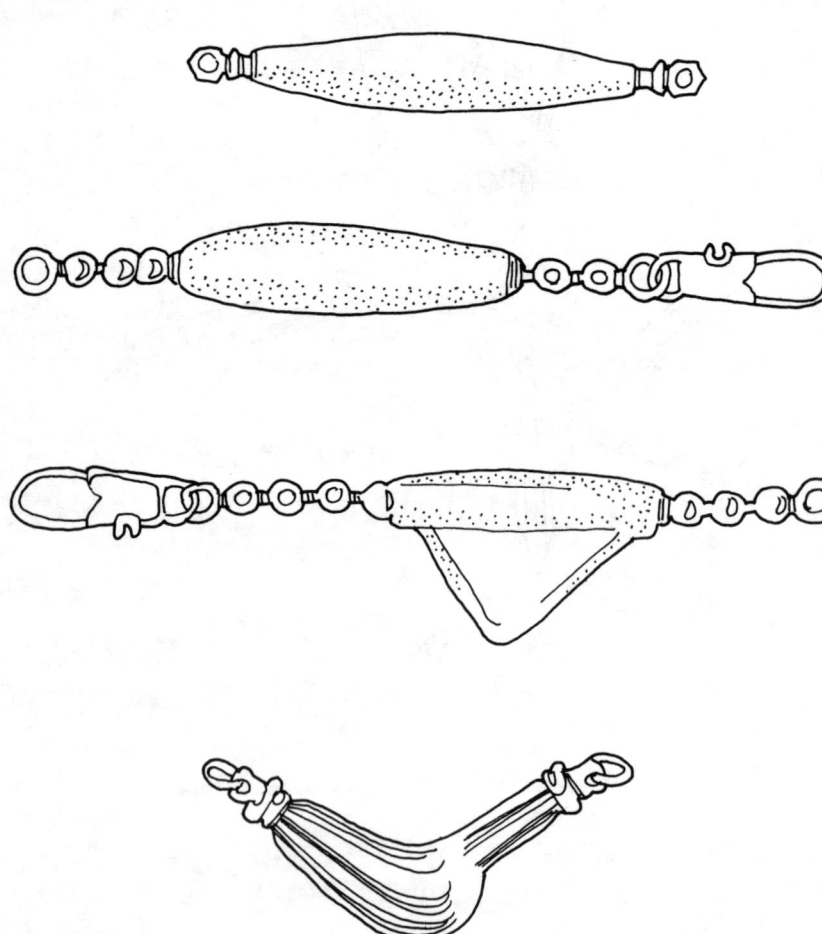

Bluefish trolling tackle should be heavy. Even small fish, when hitting lures, can put a real strain on rods and reels. Use something as heavy as a seven-foot glass rod and a conventional reel equiped with several hundred yards of forty- to sixty-pound test line. Use leaders and good quality swivels (so the line won't twist).

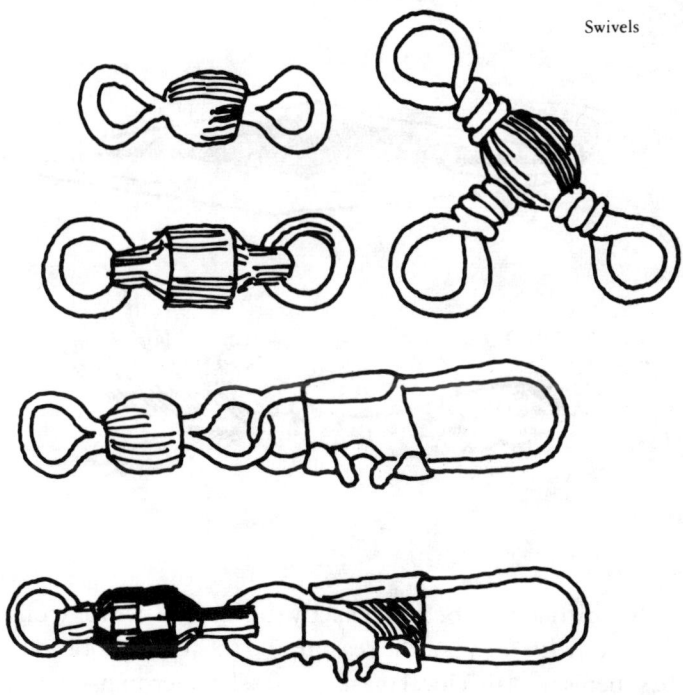

Swivels

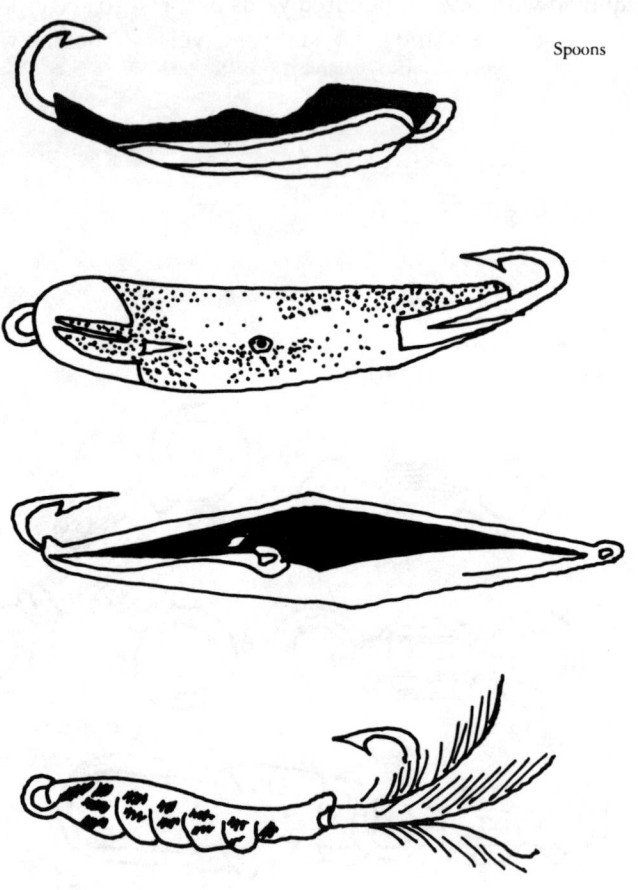

Spoons

It is difficult to spell out exactly the lures to use for trolling. It changes with the year, the season, and the fishing location. Your best bet is to visit a local marina and ask fishermen what they are using. In one part of the country, spoons might be taking fish; somewhere else it might be tubes. In general, take along a variety of lures — metal, plastic, and rubber — and try to cover all depths and speeds while you are trolling.

Trolling has been called the lazy way to fish and that is one way to approach it. You can throw over a couple of lines, put the rods in the holders, and doze your way down the beach. You may even catch fish.

But trolling is also a science and deserves thought. This means figuring out where the fish are and how to attract them, subjects covered in the previous section. One additional concern should be the proper depth for trolled lures. There are a few simple guidelines. First, the slower your boat is moving the deeper your lure will go. Also, the more line you have out the deeper your lure will be. When the fish are on the surface, fishing is fairly straightforward. You skirt the school at a good speed, keeping the lures near the surface. When no fish are showing, or when your recording shows the fish at depth, then you must get your lures down to them. Here is how to do it:

--Troll slower, or let out line.

--Use lures that dive. These are lures with extended lower "lips" which dig into the water.

--Use trolling weights or planers, devices to take your lure and line down.

--Use wire line. This line is heavier and also creates less resistance to the water and naturally drops down. But wire line (usually stainless steel) is expensive, not easy to handle, and takes special rods and guides because wire can cut, and I favor staying with standard monofilament or dacron line and using the other techniques to drop the lure.

Bluefish will take a lure trolled very fast, up to five knots. When you are hooking fish at this speed, try stopping the boat once you have a fish on. It makes catching the fish much more enjoyable. At other times, you will need to troll very slowly and very deep, almost to the point where your boat is at a standstill; in this situation, it often pays off to give the lure some added action by working the rod up and down. And, finally, you will find occasions when the blues are so deep that it makes more sense to stop the boat and jig lures — spoons, bucktails, bananas — straight up and down.

Back to fish on the surface for a moment. There will be times when a school of bluefish is hunting baitfish in a maelstrom of activity right on the surface. Instead of trolling through the school or around its edges, try stopping your boat and casting lures into the school. This way, you have a better feel of the fish, you can fish in quiet with the engine off, and you can avoid spooking the school. So always tuck a few casting rods in your boat when you go trolling.

Trolling troll.

2. BAIT FOR BLUEFISH

Bait for bluefish should be fresh, should have a fishy taste, should look like a live fish, and should move. While bluefish have been caught on almost any bait, the following are usually the best (what you use and how big a piece you use will depend upon local supply and the size of the fish around, but the general rule holds — big fish, big bait):

-- *Menhaden (bunker), mackerel:* these are the most commonly used bluefish baits (it's good oily bait). Cut the head off, and then split the fish lengthwise on either side of the backbone. The bait can be either chunked or cut in strips.

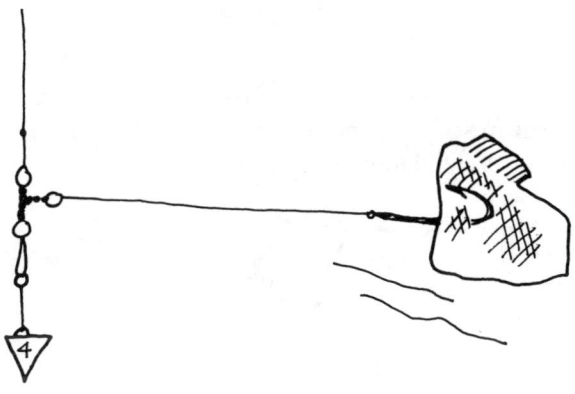

-- *Butterfish:* cut the head off, then cut the fish in two to five pieces. Cut right through the fish, so that each piece has a section of backbone in it.

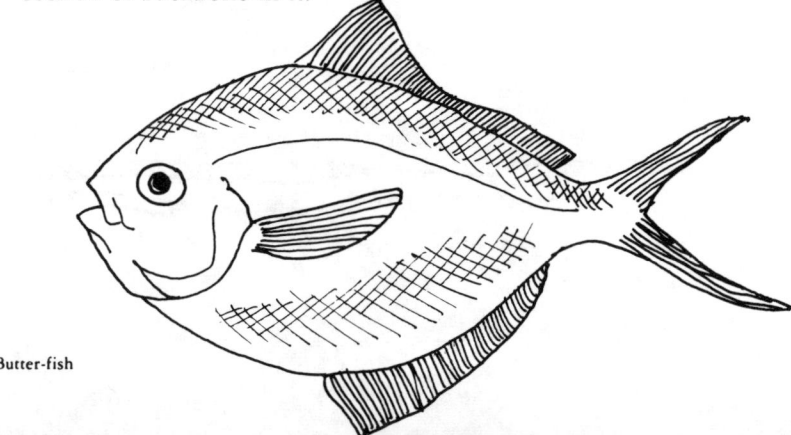

Butter-fish

-- *Mullet:* big mullet, six inches to six pounds, should be prepared like bunker or mackerel. Smaller mullet can be used whole. Buy a rig with a double hook attached to a four-inch wire with a loop on the end — (ask for it at the bait shops). Take the hook off the loop, run the wire in the mullet's mouth and out the vent, attach the hook and draw the mullet back over the hooks.

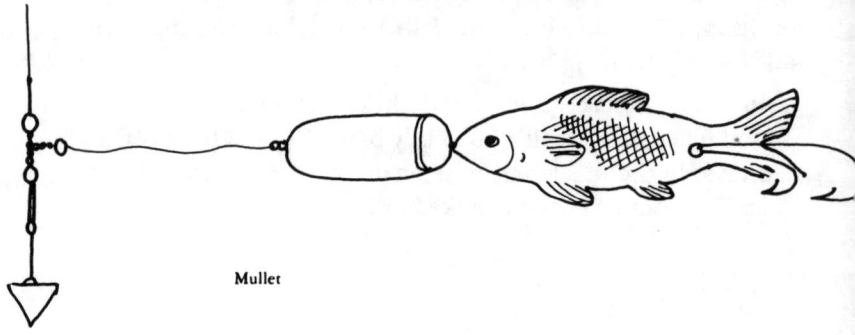

Mullet

-- *Squid:* cut in strips, a quarter to a half inch wide, and four to five inches long. Hook it on so it flutters.

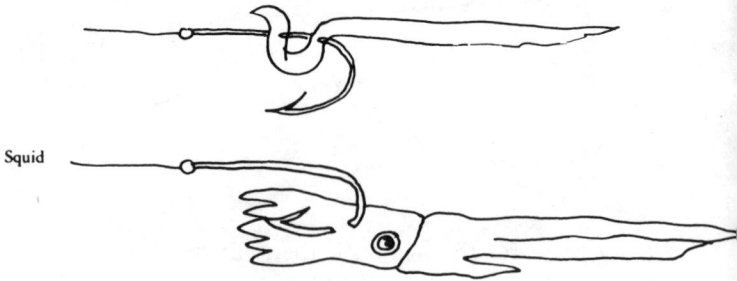

Squid

-- *Eels:* an excellent bluefish bait. Hook small ones through the mouth.

Eel

Many bait and tackle stores carry live bunker as part of their stock. It has become a favorite for blues and striped bass. Bunker can be kept alive in a large bucket with a bubbler. Don't try to keep more than three bunker alive in one bucket, however; they will use up the oxygen and die.

Bunker school throughout the summer near shore and in bays, and it is possible to catch your own for bait. One way is to locate such a school and cast a naked treble hook or a light lure with a treble hook across the school and jerk it back through, foul-hooking a bunker, usually in the back. When you have hooked one, you can stop reeling, put the reel on a free spool, and let the bunker swim along with the school. Usually your hooked bunker will fall behind or below the school, and because of its erratic swimming motions, it is often the one bunker in the bunch that a big bluefish will choose to attack.

If you are using this method but missing strikes, change tactics. If you reel in a bunker after it has been hit you might find it chopped cleanly in two, often behind the hook. Try this: when you snag a bunker, reel it in and rehook it, either right in the middle of the back or with a two-hook system. See the drawing below. This will help you catch those blues that have been chopping your bait up.

Whole live bunker will catch other fish beside blues. Let me illustrate. A friend of mine once took five blues in the 10 pound range, two 10-pound weakfish, and a pair of striped bass, one 15 pounds, the other closer to 30, all on live bunker. He had found a school of bunker trapped against a short rocky jetty. He cast a bare treble hook into the school, hooked a bunker, and let it swim. The blues got to the baits fast, but two bass tagged the baits also, and when he had hits but missed the fish, he let the remainder of the bait sink through the feeding bass and blues, and that is how he caught the weakfish. He gave me one of the weakfish to take home for supper. When I gutted it, I found two bunker heads in its belly. Apparently the weakfish, possibly as less aggressive feeders, were hanging below the feeding blues/bass, picking up the leftovers.

Bunker

3. SURF-FISHING FOR BLUEFISH

Surf-fishing for bluefish is at once the most simple and the most frustrating way to go. It is simple because all you need to do is walk down to the ocean's edge and cast out into the sea. It can be frustrating because you can spend hours without catching anything, while you watch boats offshore catching (or appearing to catch) many big blues. But if you are in the surf at the right place and the right time, you may be treated to one of the great

pleasures of fishing — the arrival of a school of bluefish that are so intent on filling their stomachs that every lure or bait that you throw out catches fish. Such surf action is often called a "blitz" — a time when bluefish come right into the surf, almost begging to be caught.

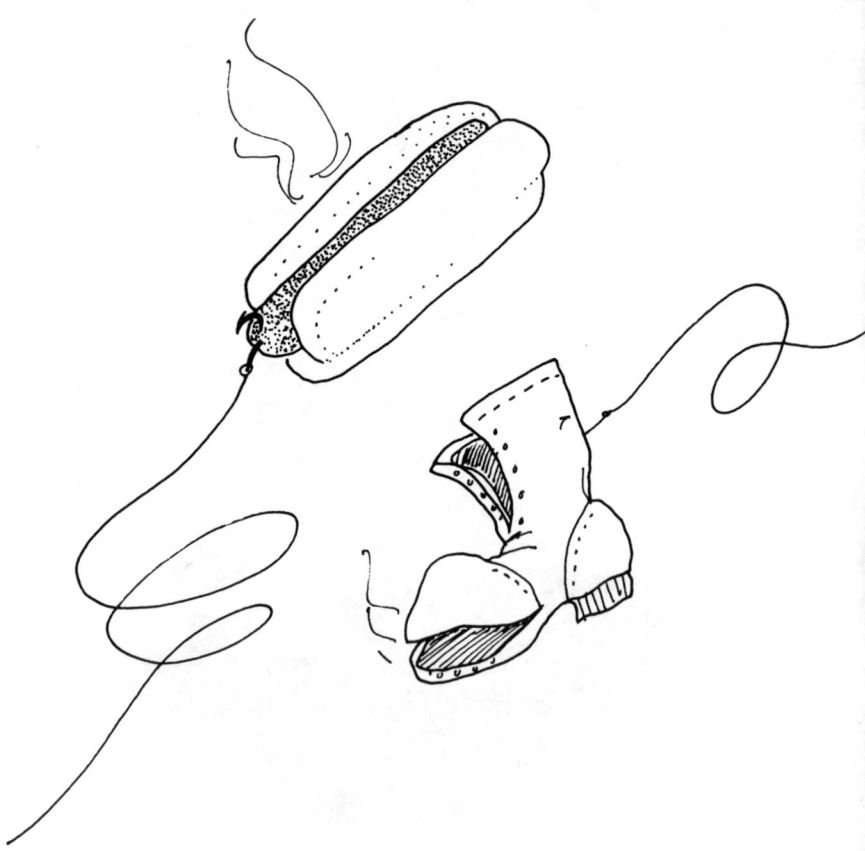

One way to be always ready for a blitz is to carry a surf-fishing rod whenever you go to the beach. Either tuck it in the trunk, or carry it on the roof of your car, or take it with you when you are going for a swim. A light surf rod and a few artificial lures take up little room.

Put together the following tackle:
-- a light, seven- to eight-foot surf rod
-- a spinning reel equipped with 200 yards of ten- to twenty-pound test line

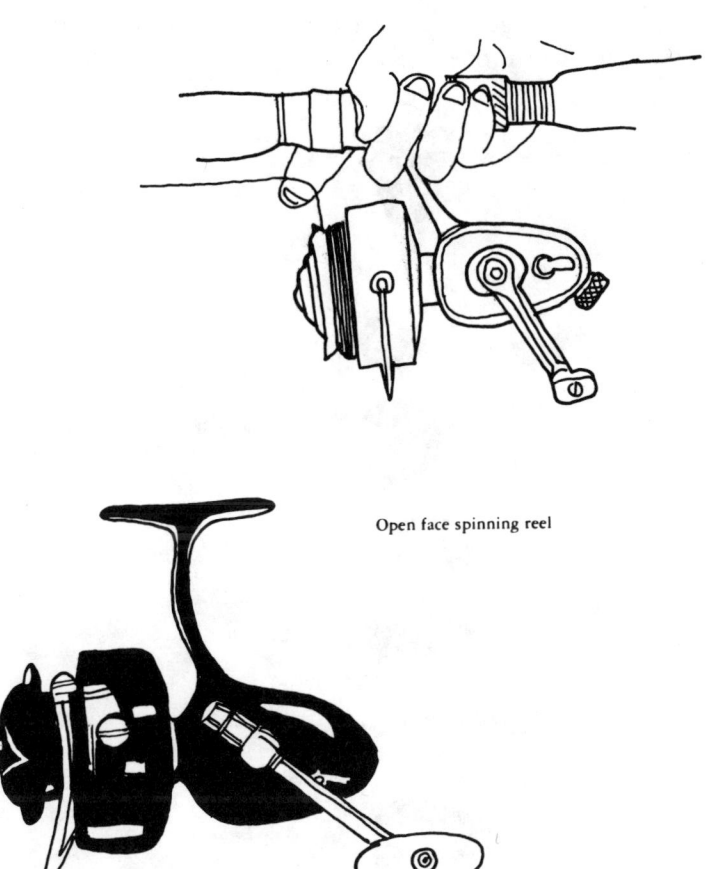

Open face spinning reel

-- an assortment of lures
-- some cut bait, as mentioned earlier
-- an assortment of weights, especially one- to three-ounce pyramid sinkers
-- a supply of two-foot leaders
-- an assortment of bait hooks

The easiest outfit to use in the surf is a one- to three-ounce pyramid sinker on the end of your line, with a floated hook on a two-foot leader attached to the line approximately three inches away from the sinker.

When bait-fishing, cast and wait; when lure-fishing, cast and reel. The best guide for surf-fishing is to use lures if the fish show, and bait if they don't.

Sinkers

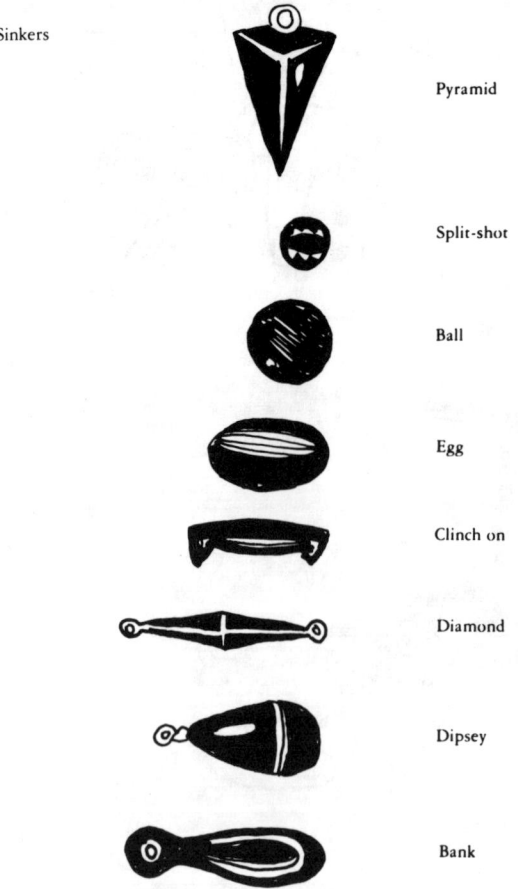

Pyramid

Split-shot

Ball

Egg

Clinch on

Diamond

Dipsey

Bank

For lures: use metal, spoons or spinners, like the Hopkins, about an ounce or so in weight; a few popping plugs (the ones that jump across the surface when retrieved); and some swimming plugs — Rebels, Bananas, or Atom Swimmers.

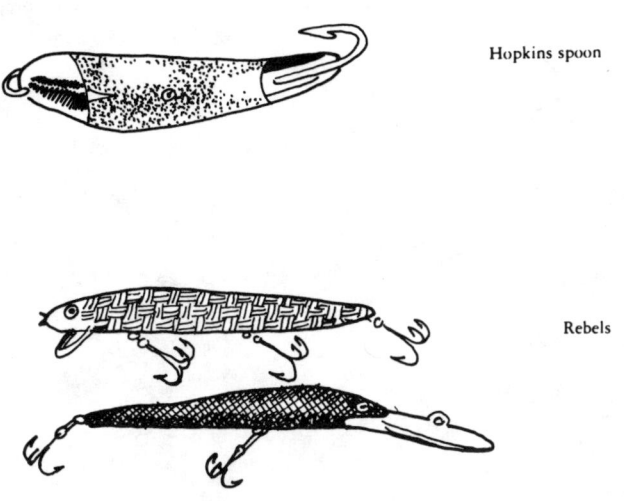

Hopkins spoon

Rebels

Bluefish seem to like shiny metal lures best, so concentrate on them. And don't let a metal lure get dull; shine it up. You can use a foot of stainless steel leaders if you want. People swear this is needed to protect against the sharp teeth of the blues, but in twenty years of surf-fishing for bluefish with lures, I have yet to have a bluefish chop off a lure.

If blues are feeding and you can see them, or if others are catching bluefish, simply get down to the water's edge and start casting. Be sure not to crowd other fishermen; but don't be afraid to see what lures or baits are catching fish, and where people are casting.

Here are some other signs of places to fish on the beach:
-- *Birds:* a fishing rule: always look for feeding birds. It doesn't always mean fish, but it's a very good sign. Watch especially for terns and small gulls, diving and screaming.

-- *Bait:* watch the surf for small baitfish jumping or swirling. There are probably fish below. Or, if you see a school of bait moving down the beach, it might be worthwhile following to see if it attracts fish. Then you can cast, but avoid casting right into the baitfish. Cast along the edges. This will not spook the bait or or the bluefish.
-- *Swirls:* sometimes fish will be feeding right under the water's surface, so you won't see the bait itself, just swirls of the feeding fish. Cast there.

If you see fish, or if you or others are catching them, then obviously that's the place to fish. But often you are on the beach and there are no signs of fish. Then you must look for them, and that means learning how to "read" the surf and the shore. It means, in a sense, "thinking" like a bluefish.

The best rule to follow is to find a place where there is an irregularity. This could be a sand bar, a point, a gully, a different pattern of waves breaking, or something jutting out from the beach — a jetty, for example. Irregularities, sand bars and such, attract baitfish. Maybe the water there surges and kicks up food. Or maybe the water behind the bar is a good place to keep out of a strong current. Often baitfish move down a beach until they get to a jetty, then gather behind the jetty out of the water's main flow. Bluefish are also known to gather at jetties, swiping at schools of bait as they gather, or when they finally decide to move.

If you see water breaking on a sandbar offshore, try casting first beyond the bar, then on top of it, and then on your side where there will be a gully of deeper water between the bar and the shore. Try the ends of gullies, where water washes down to the beach.

A good way to see a beach is to study it at low tide, perhaps even sketching the beach, the bars, and the gullies. Or, mark locations of such features above the high tide line. Then, come back at high tide and fish the promising looking spots.

If you are using lures, cover all sections of the water, and change the speed of your retrieval so the lure covers different depths. Change lures and sizes of lures. Often a smaller lure will drive bluefish to biting in an area you thought was devoid of fish. And often, after you have caught a few fish, there will be a lull in the action. Changing to a larger lure may start bluefish biting again. This is because bluefish that have been sated on smaller prey will start feeding if they see larger victims.

If you are surf-fishing at night and using bait, try moving the bait. Often that starts bluefish to biting.

When bait-fishing, you might feel a "lift" rather than a bite — a simple feeling of slack in the line. This is caused by a bluefish biting your bait while the bait is between you and the sinker. If this happens, strike back very fast to set the hook. In almost all other cases, however, the blue will hook itself without your having to set the hook.

And finally, fish sometimes feed according to tides. If you aren't having any luck, wait for a tide change.

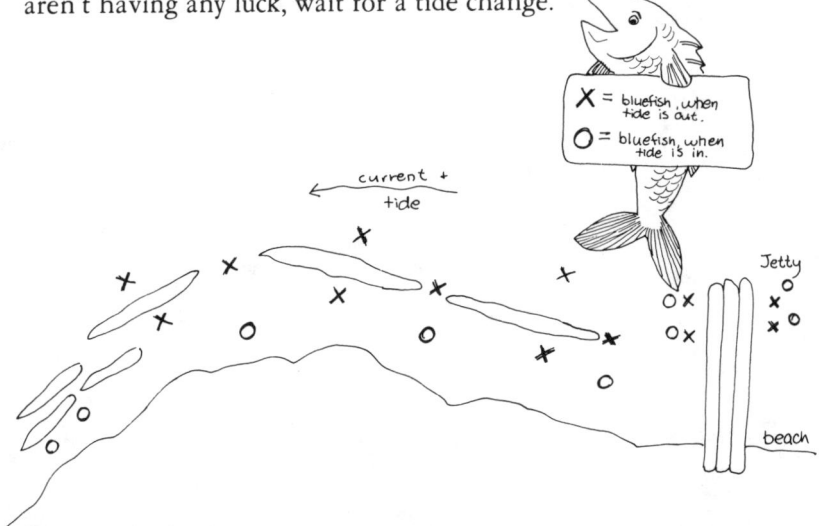

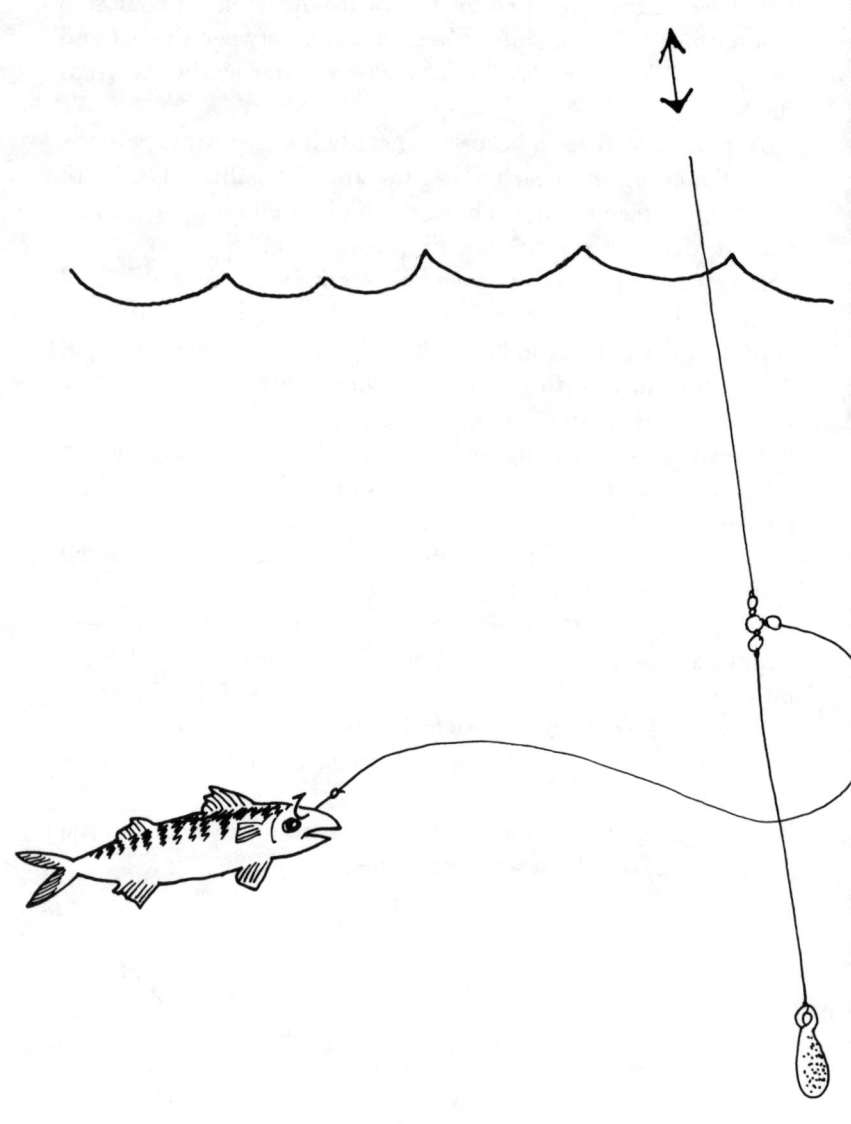

4. SNAPPERS

Fishing for Snappers

Fishing for snappers is summer fishing — a great way to spend a day in the sun and catch some supper. Baby bluefish pour into bays and estuaries in early summer to feed and grow. Usually by August they are five or six inches long, big enough to catch and eat.

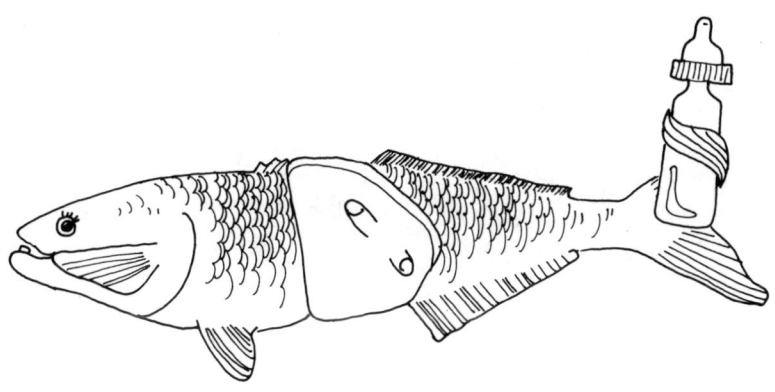

Snappers feed in schools, moving around in the water searching for small fish which they attack with abandon. They will usually flip and churn in the water when they feed, but sometimes the school is below the surface and you must fish for them blindly.

Snappers can be caught with baits or lures, and they can be caught from docks, piers, and bay banks, in which case you try to attract the fish to you. And of course you can fish from boats, in which case you can go look for the fish.

Bait-Fishing for Snappers

Use light tackle, small hooks, and live bait. Any two- to three-inch small fish such as minnows or silversides will do. The simplest rig is a long cane pole with fifteen to twenty feet of line on the end, a bobber, and a hook below the bobber. Hook the bait through the nose and mouth, or through the back in such a way

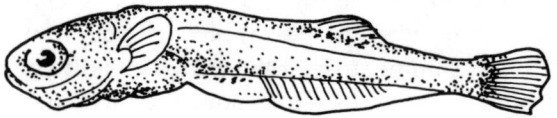

Silverside

Sheepshead minnow

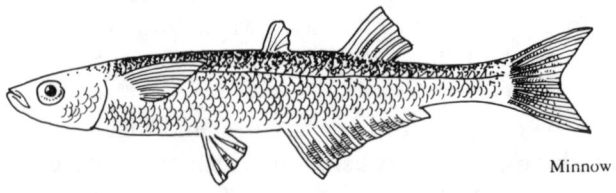

Minnow

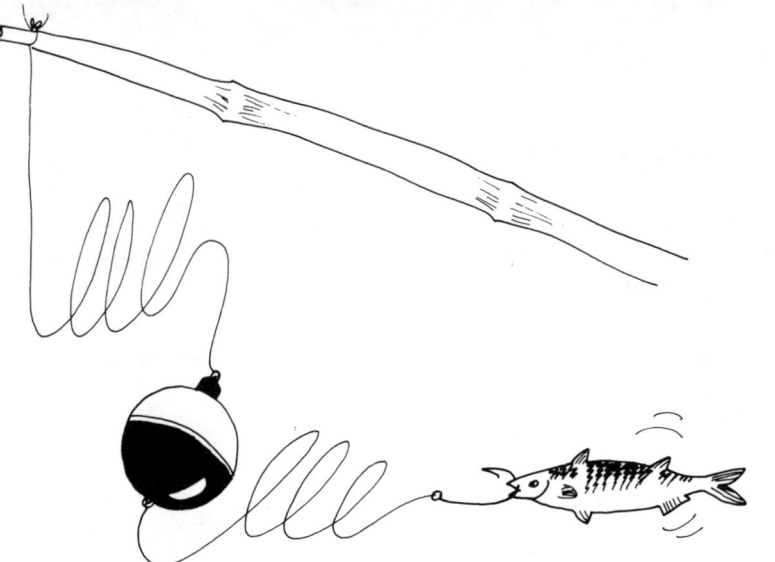

that the bait will stay alive and swim. Cast out and watch the bobber. Snappers bite or slash quickly; there won't be a little nibble, so be ready to pull back when the bobber moves. Try different places if you aren't getting bites, or take off the bobber and let the minnow swim free to find the snapper.

You can attract snappers by chumming, either by tossing over a few minnows, or by putting chopped clams, fish, or even catfood in a "chum pot" and dropping it just below the surface where you are fishing. A chum pot can be made from hardware cloth. All it has to be is a bag that you can put chum in along with a weight. Lower it into the water on a piece of string. Or use a coffee can with some holes punched in it and the plastic cover snapped back on.

Dead minnows can be used for bait if you don't have live ones, and sometimes they work just as well. If your dead minnows don't catch fish standing still, try moving them.

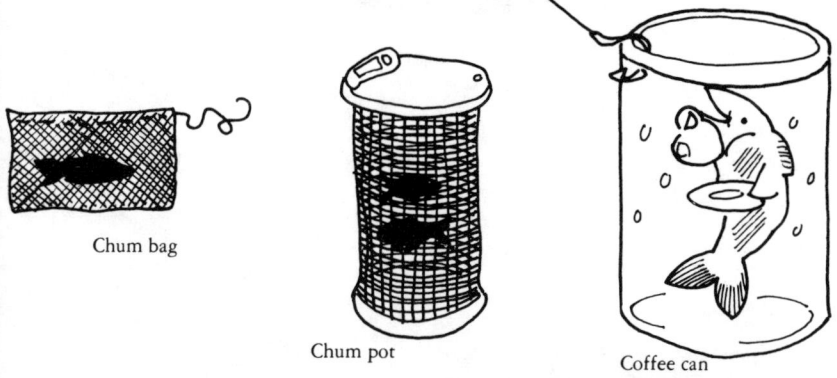

Chum bag

Chum pot

Coffee can

Using Lures

When snappers are on a feeding binge, you can catch them with small spinners, spoons, and wobblers, or almost any small, shiny lure. The best size is from one to three inches long.

If you are fishing for snappers from a boat without luck, try trolling until you find a school, then you can stop and cast for them.

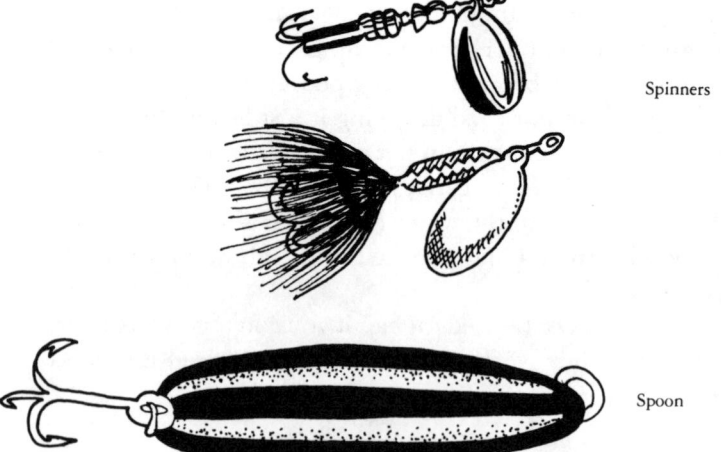

Spinners

Spoon

5. KEEPING AND CLEANING YOUR CATCH

To preserve their flavor, all fish should be handled with care, but especially bluefish, because their digestive juices are strong, and because they are a fatty fish.

Bluefish should be cleaned and iced as soon as possible. Even if you cannot ice them immediately, cleaning them will help preserve the meat. You don't have to interrupt fishing each time you catch one, but if you have caught a few and there is a lull in the action, take the time to clean your fish.

I call the following method "field" or "boat" or "beach" cleaning. This is just an interim step done while you are fishing; the final cleaning is done at the end of the day.

To clean a bluefish, lay it on its side and place your hand on top of the fish to steady it. Insert a sharp knife into the fish's vent (anus) and draw the knife forward, right up to the head. Reach into the cavity and remove the entrails. (This is a good time to cut open the stomach and see what the bluefish has been eating. You

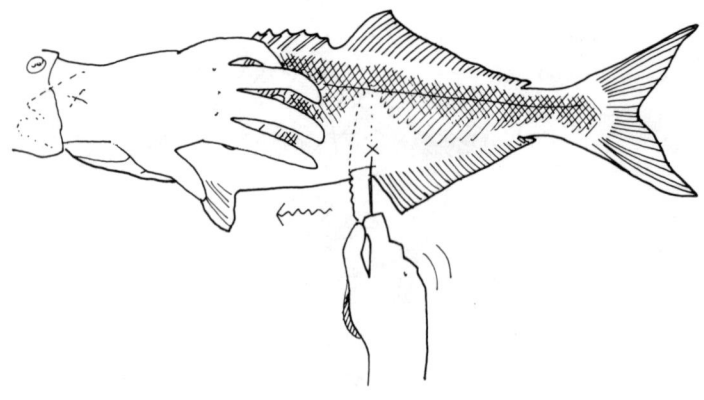

may want to change your bait or lure.) The entrails will be attached to the body near the head — cut them free. Then run your thumbnail or the tip of the knife along the top of the interior cavity, removing the blood there. Rinse the cavity and the fish quickly, and ice it as soon as you can.

If you are on the beach and cannot ice your fish right away, bury it in the sand a foot or so down. The sand is cooler there even on a hot day. Mark the place where you have buried your fish. I recommend not cleaning the fish before you bury it, or you will have fish that will be next to impossible to rinse free of sand.

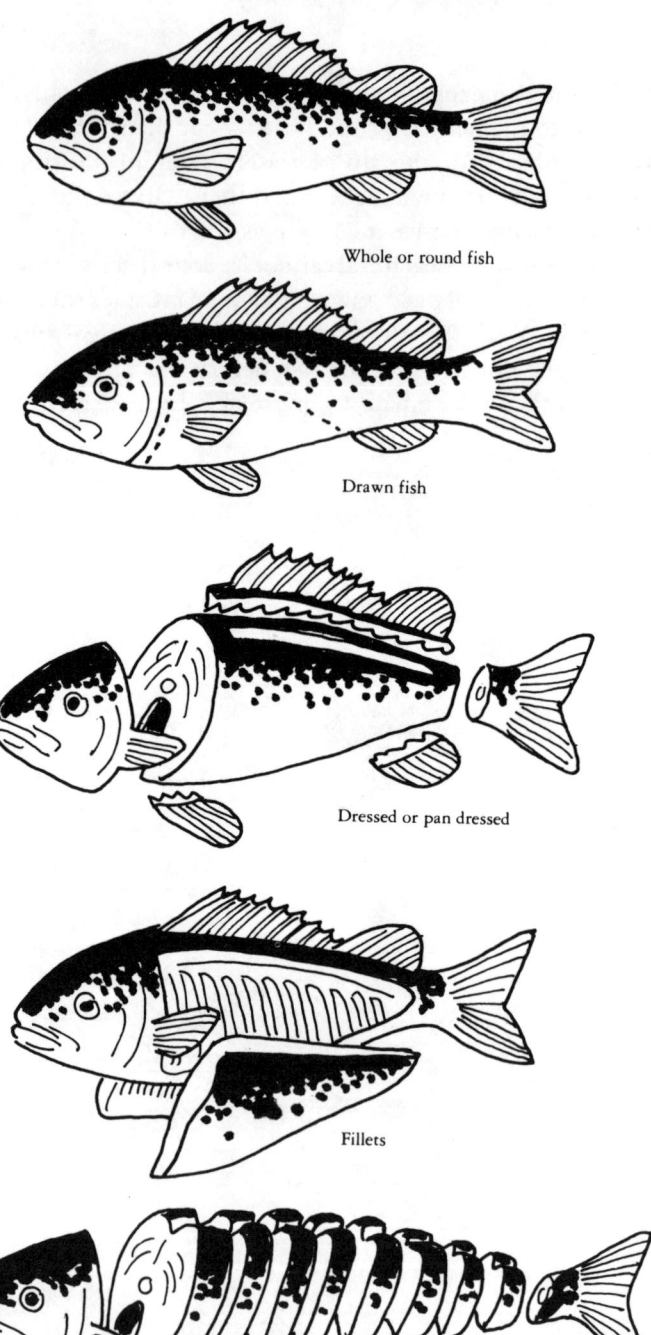

You can also carry a stringer and keep your fish in the water with you as you wade in the surf. Above all, keep your bluefish from getting warm or dry.

So! You have kept the fish in good condition out in the field (or water), and now you are back at the house with half a dozen nice fat field-dressed bluefish, chilled and glistening. Preparing a fish — cleaning it, dressing it, or whatever it's called — is not difficult. If you have never cleaned a fish, try following these directions. Better yet, watch an experienced fisherman and ask her or him to describe the process. Here's how:

The fish should be damp; a dried out fish is hard to scale. If it's dry, soak the fish for a few minutes in cool water. You can either scale or completely skin a bluefish. If you are scaling the fish, do it with the head on; the head provides something to hold while working. Place the fish on its side and run a scaler or knife against the grain of the scales, using a back and forth motion, from tail to head. Fresh, moist, small fish should scale with ease. Bigger fish and dry fish take more work. Rinse the fish well after you have scaled it.

Let's continue:

1. Cut the fish's head off right behind the gills. This will probably produce some blood but don't panic unless it's your own.

2. If the fish has not been cleaned in the field, do that now. Refer to the section on field cleaning if necessary.

3. If the fish is small and you want to cook it whole, you are ready to go.

4. If it's a large fish, you will probably want to split it. To split it, complete steps one and two, then lie the fish on its side, dorsal or top fin facing you. Place your knife against the backbone and cut lengthwise straight back. Turn the fish over and repeat. You will have two pieces of meat and a backbone. You can cut the rib bones out of the meat if you wish.

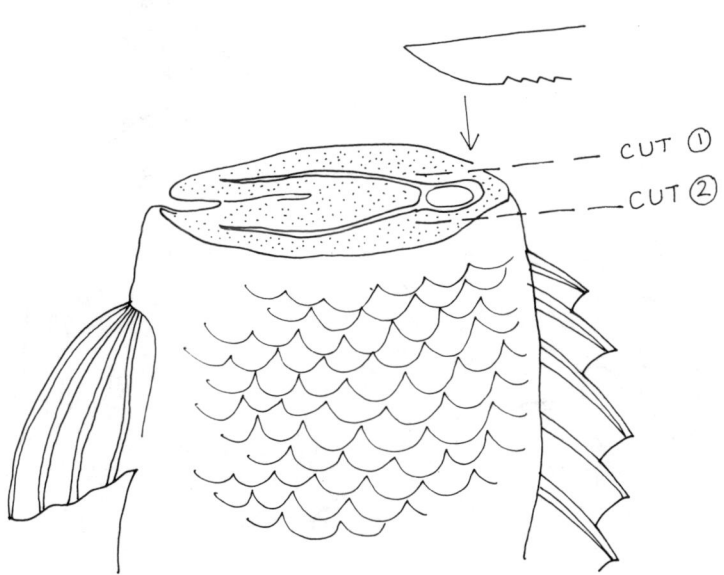

5. Don't rinse the fish after this step, or you will wash away a great deal of flavor. Pat the fish dry. Fresh bluefish can be kept in a refrigerator for a day or so without losing much flavor, but try to cook and eat your fish as soon as possible after it has been caught.

6. If you want to skin your bluefish (and some think the skin of a fish makes it too strong tasting) lay the half fish skin down, tail end to your left (if you're righthanded). Hold the fish down with your left thumb, just half an inch from the small end. Cut down through the meat to the skin right in front of your grip, then turn the knife flat against the skin with the sharp edge facing the head end of the fish. Now, with the knife flat against the skin, pull the fish away from the knife with your left hand while moving the knife gently to and fro in a sawing motion. You will cut away the skin as the knife moves toward the head.

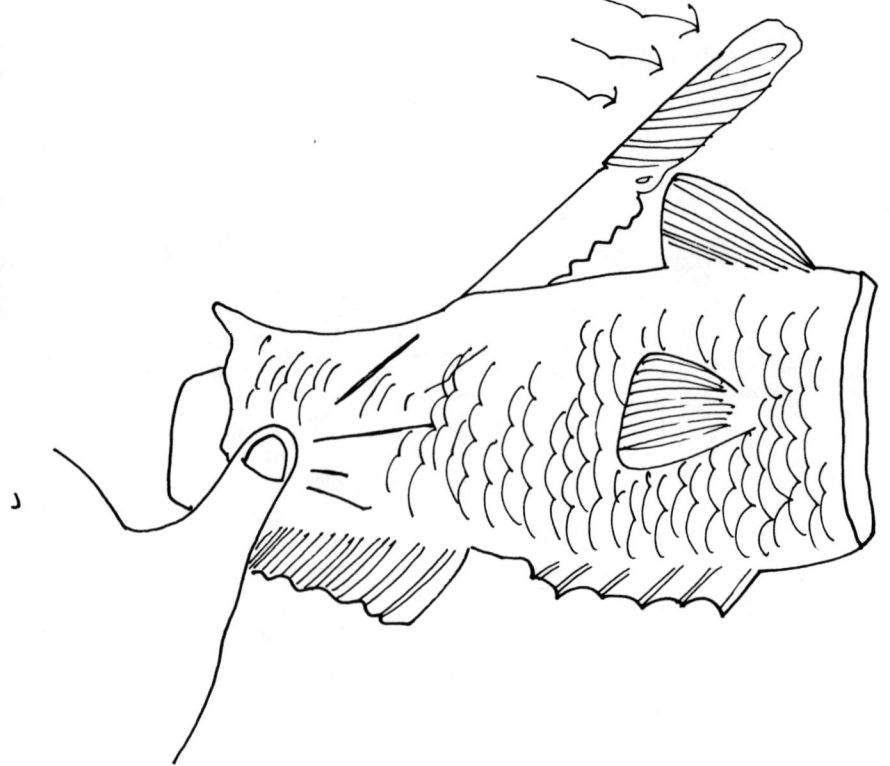

7. One last tip: to remove the smell from your hands, wash them in cold water and then rub them with two tablespoons of table salt. Rinse again in cold water. Most of the smell will go away.

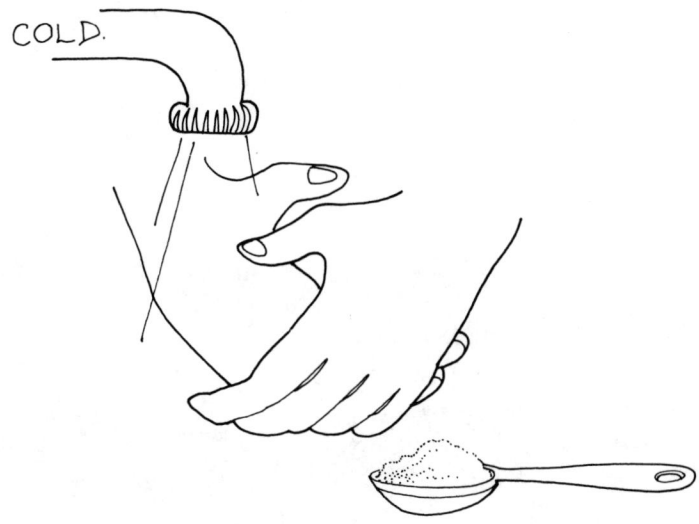

6. COOKING BLUEFISH

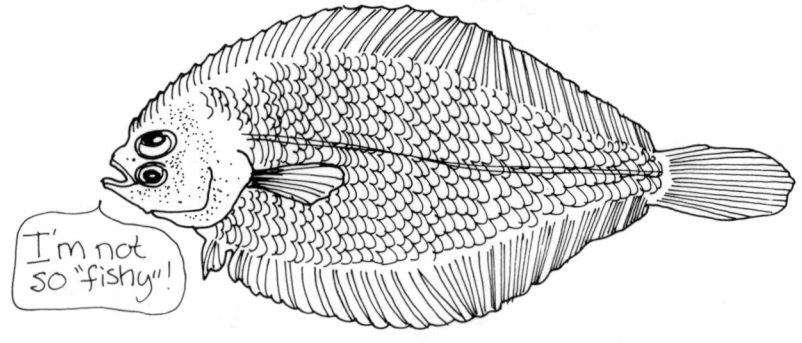

Bluefish are good eating if you like the taste of fish. That sounds funny, but some people don't like "fishy" fish. If you prefer a bland tasting fish like flounder, you might find bluefish a little strong. But give freshly caught bluefish a try and then decide. One important guide: don't overcook fish; it gets dry, tough, and tasteless. Properly cooked fish is moist and flaky. Cook it only until it loses its translucency; the meat should just have turned white.

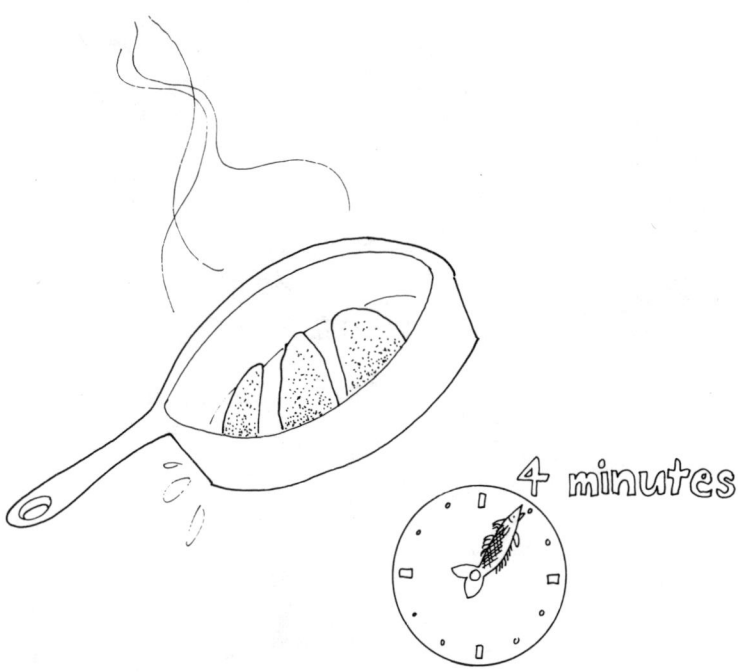

Fried Bluefish

This is a good, easy way to cook snappers or halves of small fish, up to approximately three pounds.

Dip the fish lightly in bread crumbs and fry in butter or oil in a hot pan, four minutes on a side. Have a batch of them; it's easy to toss down five to ten snappers at a sitting.

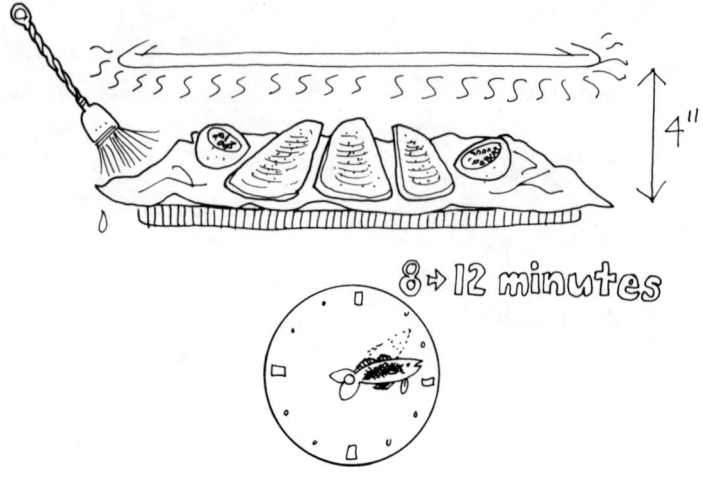

Oven-Broiled Bluefish

Turn on the broiler full blast and set the rack four inches below the flame. Place halves of fish skin-side down on the broiler tray, or on a piece of foil that has been lightly oiled. Baste with butter, oil, or french dressing. Add lemon, salt and pepper, and cook for eight to twelve minutes. The top should have a light crust on it. (Try broiling a few tomatoes at the same time. Cut them in half and sprinkle with oregano, celery salt, and pepper.)

Bluefish Baked in Milk

    This recipe will provide fish lovers with a great change of pace. It's delicious and it's easy to prepare.
    Layer the fish in a casserole dish. Add milk or half-and-half until the fish is almost covered. Cover the fish with a layer of thickly sliced sharp cheddar cheese and bake for one hour at 350 degrees. In another casserole dish, I usually scallop some potatoes or tomatoes at the same time, and serve with warm dinner rolls or hard bread.

Bluefish Soup

Bluefish makes good strong soup. Make a broth by boiling three pounds of heads and backbones in two quarts of water. Boil for ten minutes and then pick out and reserve what meat you can from the bones to be added later. Put the head back in the pot and boil for another fifty minutes with two bay leaves, a little salt, and plenty of pepper. Strain the broth, and you have an excellent soup.

If you want a clear soup, just add carrots, celery, and tomatoes. Just before serving, add the meat you have reserved and bring just to a boil.

For a good chowder, add potatoes and bring to a boil. When potatoes are tender, add lightly fried onions, a tablespoon of butter, and, just before serving, a cup of cream or milk and the meat you have saved.

Bluefish on the Grill

Bluefish cooks great on charcoal. It's my favorite way. Get one of those "sandwich" grills used for hamburgers — one you can put the fish on and turn. Baste the fish with a sauce of your choosing — barbecue sauce, garlic butter, or french dressing are all good. Turn the fish a few times until it gets a little crusty on each side. Test with a fork; it should be flaky. Serve it with potato salad or cole slaw, french bread heated on the grill, and a simple cool white wine. Superb at sunset!

Baked Bluefish

This is my favorite recipe for cooking big blues, from six to fifteen pounds. The fish should be cleaned, scaled, rinsed and patted dry. I leave the head on unless it needs to be removed to get the fish in the oven.

Stuff the stomach with a mixture of chopped onions, tomatoes, peppers, bread crumbs, salt and pepper. Wrap the fish tightly in foil and bake for an hour at 350 degrees. Serve with baked potatoes and a green salad. Make it a point to open the fish wrap at the table; the burst of aroma is guaranteed to make your mouth water.

Leftover baked fish makes good salad. Flake the chilled meat and mix it the way you would tuna fish.

Smoked Bluefish

Bluefish smokes very well. Take fish that have been headed and cleaned but not split. Soak twelve hours in a brine solution (one-eighth cup salt per quart of water). Remove the fish, drain it, pat it dry, and leave it in the air for an hour to dry further. Place it in a smoker, following the directions on the smoker for either hot or cold smoke. I allow eight hours of hot smoke for a four- to eight-pound bluefish. However, smoking does not preserve the fish. It merely cooks it and gives it flavor. To keep, it should be refrigerated if it is to be eaten within a week, or frozen if it is to kept longer.

Here's another smoking preparation: add to a large plastic bag one-quarter cup salt and one-half cup brown sugar. Add fish and shake well. Tie the bag shut and leave overnight. The next day, remove the fish, wipe dry, and smoke as before. This makes a flavorful, colorful smoke. The fish is darker and has a more pungent quality.

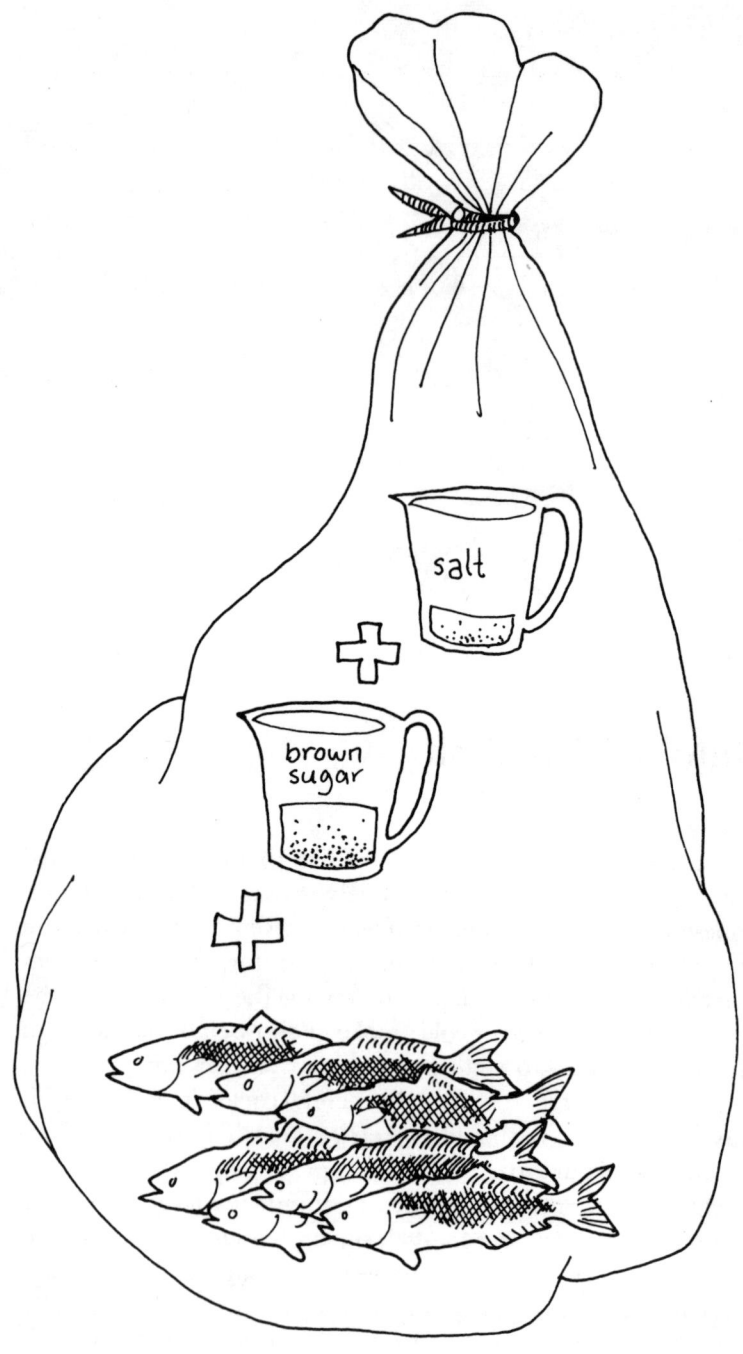

Some Final Cooking Tips:

-- If you find bluefish too strong for your taste, remove the dark meat along each side of the backbone (you will see it after you split the fish). This is especially helpful with big bluefish.

-- You can freeze bluefish, but it does not keep as well or as long as other less fatty fish. Try to eat fish that have been frozen within a month. And freeze only fresh fish that have been skinned. Smoked fish can be frozen too.

-- Remember the cardinal rules for all fish, and especially bluefish

— keep your catch cool and moist

— eat as soon after catching as possible

— don't overcook.

Have a good meal!

In Conclusion

Here are some suggestions and reminders that will lead to better bluefishing:

-- Fish whenever you can. The fisherman who catches the most fish is the one with his hook in the water. You can't catch fish dreaming about them in front of the television set, or hanging around the bait shop trading stories.

-- All other things being equal, fish at sunrise and sunset.

-- Watch other successful fishermen and ask them questions. They are usually willing to share what they know.

-- Don't crowd other fishermen. Give them elbow room.

-- Keep a fishing diary. I have a simple five-year diary. Each time I fish I note times, weather, tides, where I went, what I caught and didn't catch, lures, and baits. Diaries are good for recalling last year's patterns of fish movements. Also, reading a diary in mid-winter is a good way to warm up, especially if there is a wood stove nearby.

-- Bluefish are sometimes possible to catch in huge numbers. During a blitz you may be able to catch a fish on every cast. Just remember, for every fish you kill, you need a seafood lover to eat it. So don't take more than you can use. Leave some for other fishermen and other days.

-- And, one last time, be careful of a bluefish's teeth. Bluefish can and will bite the hand that catches them — they can hurt.

Good luck!

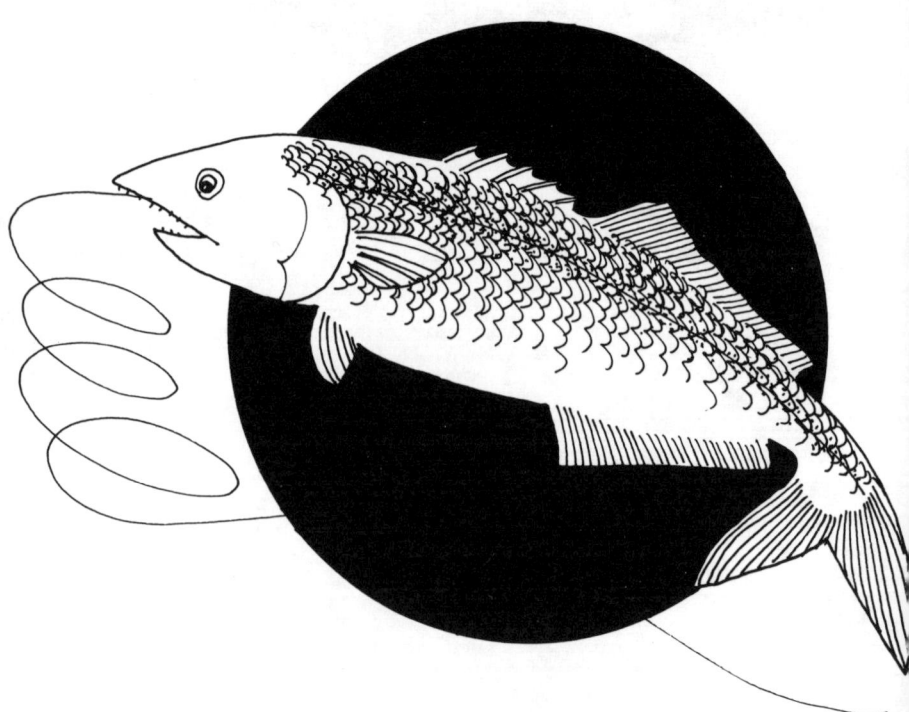

Notes
GOOD RECORDS MAKE FOR GOOD CATCHES.

Notes

Notes

Notes

Notes

Notes